12 Rules for Jiu Jitsu

A Commentary on Jordan Peterson's
12 Rules for Life

Chris Matakas

OTHER BOOKS BY CHRIS MATAKAS

My Mastery: Learning To Live Through Jiu Jitsu

My Mastery: Continued Education Through Jiu Jitsu

The Tao of Jiu Jitsu

On Jiu Jitsu

5 Rules For White Belts

12 Rules For Jiu Jitsu: A Commentary on
Jordan Peterson's *12 Rules For Life*
Copyright ©2018 by Chris Matakas
Ferryman Publishing
ISBN-13: 978-1720850434
ISBN-10: 1720850437
Edited by Kathy Matakas
Cover Design by Emy Rothenberger
Back Cover Photo by Eric Talerico

FERRYMAN PUBLISHING

Disclaimer

Consider this the first ever Jiu Jitsu book report.

This work is not meant to be a replacement for Jordan Peterson's *12 Rules for Life*. This book is a commentary on how those rules are applicable to our experiences using Jiu Jitsu as a vehicle for personal development.

Within this text, there are many quotes from Peterson with my personal interpretations of them. My conclusions are not representative of Peterson's opinions but rather expressions of my own. Unless otherwise noted, all quotes are from *12 Rules For Life*.

Jordan Peterson was not involved in the making of this book. This book is not representative of Jordan Peterson or his beliefs.

I have used the same chapter titles as *12 Rules for Life* for coherence.

I strongly encourage the reader to study Jordan Peterson directly. Peterson's teachings have improved my life along with the lives of millions of viewers and readers. I am grateful for his work and the courage with which he stands up for the betterment of Being.

This book is an extension of that gratitude.

CONTENTS

WHY WRITE THIS BOOK

With each book I write, I strive to articulate the beauty of Jiu Jitsu and its application as a tool for personal development. My life has grown in proportion to the sincerity of my practice -- physically, mentally, spiritually, and emotionally -- the more time I spend on the mat, the deeper I come to know myself.

A large portion of my study off the mat comes from books. Reading has become a daily constant, a must with which I start each day with more consistency and urgency than breakfast. Great books inform me how to live, and I do my best to embody their lessons on the mats each night with my teammates.

Most of my reading consists of dead philosophers and theologians. I've often felt that there are few new thoughts and the best ideas were stated long ago. And then I heard Jordan Peterson speak. His teachings are an amalgamation of the humanities -- a cohesive blend of philosophy, religion, and mythology discussed through a psychological lens. With a simplicity of language uncommon in academia, he has made archetypal ideas accessible. Peterson teaches us to aim higher, that we are not what we could be, and if we just "sorted ourselves out," our lives, the lives of those around us, and the world would improve.

After watching all the lectures his YouTube channel had to offer, I read Peterson's first book *Maps of*

Meaning. A hyper-dense and expansive read, my progress was slow: it took four months to complete and some days I couldn't read more than a few paragraphs without a loss in comprehension. I have spent a large portion of my life reading good books, and I soon realized that much of what I hoped to learn from them could be found in this single work, if only I had the focus and sincerity to truly understand what he was saying.

But it was a profundity, deep down, I already possessed. We all do. When I read his work and listen to his lectures, I am constantly struck with the sense of: I knew that, but I did not know I knew it. This is what makes something archetypal -- it touches on the deepest and truest aspects of the human experience that are applicable to our own subjective experience.

I have been studying Peterson's work for only a few years, but my life has improved to the extent that I have understood his teachings. He teaches personal development. And he does so through the greatest wisdom our written history has to offer. Undoubtedly an over-generalization, but sufficient for our purposes, his basic schema can be summarized as:

We view the world as a forum for action through the subjective lens of our goal. Therefore, we had better aim at something worthwhile. Embodying the archetype of the hero, we are to walk the tightrope between order and chaos, as we voluntarily confront the unknown to shape ourselves and our world. We aim at the star we can see, and daily strive toward that worthy ideal until we find something better to aim at. We use the commonplace routines of our lives as vehicles for this betterment, constantly striving for that heavenly city on the hill. We must aim up, as each of us possesses a sovereignty, a divinity, that improves the world to the degree that we manifest our latent potential.

Jiu Jitsu has become the lens through which I experience the world. It is my map, the schema through which I interpret and make sense of the events of life. A constant source of metaphor and understanding, the parallels between the gentle art and a life of personal development are endless -- and the deeper I understand this discipline, the richer my experience becomes.

It is this most fundamental lens which led to this book.

Peterson's *12 Rules For Life* is an accessible synthesis of his teachings, a broad generalization of the many topics discussed in his lectures and *Maps of Meaning*. Chock full of pragmatic injunctions, this book offers the reader a bridge into the mind of Peterson and the seemingly endless practical wisdom he possesses. While reading, I found myself repeatedly asking:

How can I apply these lessons to Jiu Jitsu?

The lessons were so universal that they applied directly to our practice on the mats. I knew that many improvements could be made to my community, and the Jiu Jitsu community at large, from the teachings described in this text.

My life's work has been to study great teachings and apply these lessons in the Jiu Jitsu academy -- to strive toward my highest self, and help my students do the same, by using Jiu Jitsu as a vehicle for personal development. This book is one more attempt to take these lessons off the pages and onto the mat.

Peterson's *12 Rules For Life* is a great work. This book is not meant to take its place on your bookshelf. You would be doing yourself, and the world, a disservice. Go read that book. This book, however, is an analysis of how these lessons apply to Jiu Jitsu.

I have written much about using Jiu Jitsu as a vehicle for personal development. Peterson uses every moment of our lives, especially the daily routines we rarely think about, as such a vehicle. Every experience is an opportunity to move our lives toward order, to aim up and sort ourselves out. Nothing is wasted. Everything matters. And we are all connected. When we improve ourselves, the world around us improves as well. Our efforts tangibly affect the lives of our friends, family, and community. Whether we improve or decline, the world follows our lead.

We have a responsibility to everyone else to be better.

The more sincerely we seek to embody the following lessons, the deeper and more meaningful our lives will become as we cultivate the strength to confront chaos and transform it into "habitable order."

Jordan Peterson has many of the tools we will need, and there is no better place to start applying them than on the mat.

Rule 1
Stand Up Straight With Your Shoulders Back

The chapter begins with lobsters. Lobsters exists within dominance hierarchies and share similar neurochemistry to humans. Jordan Peterson, in his talks and now this book, has used these crustaceans as proof of the existence, and therefore need, of dominance hierarchies in nature. And despite external appearances, we are still in a state of nature.

Lobsters, and the dominance hierarchies they use to organize themselves, have existed for hundreds of millions of years. When a lobster wins a fight, it postures up as serotonin flows through its veins. When it loses, it looks defeated, sunken, depressed. The lobster that wins the exchange is granted the benefits of better potential mates, more habitable space, and greater opportunities for food.

> "To those who have everything, more will be given; from those who have nothing, everything will be taken."- Matthew 25:29

Unequal distribution is a law of nature. We all start with the same resources when we play the board game Monopoly. But the game never ends that way. Invariably, winning begets winning until one player has all the resources. The momentum of progress fuels more progress, and the same holds true for Jiu Jitsu.

It Gets Easier

I have a friend who is a lifelong martial artist. Having earned multiple black belts and owning multiple martial arts schools, he possesses the gift of experience. He is constantly reminding me of the perils of familiarity with the term "black belt eyes," which denotes not what an advanced practitioner can see, but rather, what he can't. The black belt, a symbol of experience and battle-tested hypotheses, develops a lens that easily forgets the obstacles of the beginning student.

I have been training for a decade. This pales in comparison to the depth of my teacher's study but is sufficient in length for me to forget much of the experience of the uninitiated student. So I listen, and my new students help me see what I forgot long ago.

Enter Dan, a forty-something father of two recently enrolled in the program. After suffering through the initial hurdle of his first class, he has trained almost every day for the past month. At the end of each class, he marvels at how much easier each day becomes. The warm-up becomes less tiring. The hip toss feels lighter. And his water break, a once welcomed reprieve from the fatigue of training, is now non-existent. He has lost ten pounds, and this is only the beginning.

For Dan, each class has gotten better than the last. But the class has not changed. He has. He is an embodiment of this Matthew Principle. The class is not less. He is more. And this growth, and the advantages that come with it, will carry on well into black belt.

The further you go into this art, the more accessible its intricacies become. With more mat time comes a deeper understanding of the fundamental principles which underlie good grappling. As we learn more, our ability to learn increases, thus making more learning inevitable. This feedback loop continues in perpetuity.

This growth is accompanied by increased opportunity. Senior students are given leadership roles by being partnered with the new students in class. Our senior students are very much akin to assistant coaches: shouldering this greater responsibility, being the ferryman who guides the uninitiated to understanding. This serving another serves their own interest, as helping others acquire knowledge facilitates their own acquisition.

By teaching, we are forced to make our inarticulate knowledge articulate, and we begin to consciously understand what our body knows but our mouths fail to say. This is when we begin to truly understand the art as articulate knowledge translates into increased technical abilities.

Ascending this hierarchy of skill presents another gift: you can hand pick your training partners. As a norm, junior students show respect by not asking senior students to train. The senior student can choose his roles for the day based on his desires for the day. This is a necessary perk for experienced grapplers who have sacrificed much health to ascend the belt rank, and despite the belt on their waist may not have the physical ability to train with the twenty-something wrestler.

The better you get at Jiu Jitsu, the more is given to you: whether it's leadership responsibilities, continued education, or the ability to pick the training partners that most coincide with the achievement of your individual goals, increased competency means greater opportunities.

Confidence

> "The part of our brain that keeps track of our position in the dominance hierarchy is therefore exceptionally ancient and fundamental."

I have few memories from my first years of training, but I distinctly remember my first class after receiving the third stripe on my white belt. We used to get a new belt for each promotion at white belt, with each "stripe" being a blue line running through the middle, like the current kid's belt system. With each promotion came a new belt with another blue stripe, so that over time our belts gradually became more blue and less white. The three-stripe white belt was a big deal because it was the first of these belts that was more blue than white. It was representative that the student was past the halfway point.

It felt good around my waist. I remember my first warm-up lap while wearing that belt. I stood up straight. My shoulders were back. I felt pride for my accomplishment.

> "There is an unspeakably primordial calculator, deep within you, at the very foundation of your brain, far below your thoughts and feelings. It monitors exactly where you are positioned in society..."

I have learned a healthy respect for biology. That counter is real. And while on the Jiu Jitsu mat, we are all color-coded to demonstrate our position within that society. It feels good to wear a black belt. I am honored to wear a black belt. I have sacrificed much to deserve it. And over the years I have seen so many high achievers in business, sport, and life be brought to tears when awarded their blue belt. These promotions matter. Because Jiu Jitsu matters.

We understand the worth of this endeavor, and with so few tangible signs acknowledging our progress, each promotion carries great meaning. They are permanent advancements. Once you receive a black belt in Jiu Jitsu, you are a black belt in Jiu Jitsu. Forever. We wear that belt each day, always reminded of our accomplishment and striving to be worthy of it.

We share chemistry with the lobster. Serotonin modulates our well-being.

> "Low serotonin means less happiness, more pain and anxiety, more illness, and a shorter lifespan -- among humans, just as among crustaceans."

Within a Jiu Jitsu academy, a high rank gives us higher levels of serotonin. These belts feel good to wear. Not because some magic cloth wrapped around your waist leaks good vibes. It's for what the belt represents. It's recognition of who you've become, and it's who you've become that allows you to stand up tall with your shoulders back. It is my experiences in Jiu Jitsu that allow me to feel comfortable in a crowd, knowing who I am and that I have the physical and mental tools to defend myself. This resolve becomes all-encompassing, as what we become in one area of our lives invariably affects the rest of our being.

Peterson goes on to talk about positive feedback loops, citing the formation of agoraphobia in a woman, as bad experience after bad experience compound together until she can no longer muster the strength to go to the mall.

> "To forestall panic, she avoids the stress of the mall and returns home. But now the anxiety systems in her brain note that she ran away from the mall and conclude that the journey there was truly dangerous."

This is another concept that I have come to understand through Peterson. When you define something as a great obstacle or threat, you are also defining yourself as something small, incapable of surmounting it. We know this from our dreams. When you run away from danger, that which causes your fear grows and you shrink. Conversely, when you directly face the problem, going into the belly of the whale, you grow and the monster shrinks.

We must face what we've been avoiding. When we put off all the little chores of the day, we build them up and tacitly define ourselves as unable to confront them. Luckily, this form of delay is antithetical to the practice of Jiu Jitsu.

Jiu Jitsu forces us to daily confront the dragon to win the gold. By seeking growth, we must risk failure. We are constantly on the edge of our competence as we seek to acquire new skills. We fail repeatedly in the process. But we see failure as necessary on the path to success. We do not imagine ourselves to be without flaws. We are more aware than that. We define ourselves, to quote Peterson:

> "...as the being who constantly realizes his flaws and overcomes them."

This is the source of true confidence and the gift Jiu Jitsu provides. We are forced to embody this growth mindset in which we continually confront our

18

shortcomings and overcome them. And by doing this on the mat, we do it in our world.

My life has grown in proportion to my skill as a martial artist. My health has improved (sort of). I have pursued writing. An intimate relationship. Started my own business. All these new roles are made possible by the lessons I have learned on the mat which have engrained the need to risk failure if I am to achieve true success. Jiu Jitsu has given me a strength with which to confront my daily experience. And it's the times I have competed on the mats or fought in the ring that have given me the strength and confidence to not have to prove that strength in the world.

A Good Person

"If you can bite, you generally don't have to."

The toughest dudes I know are the kindest dudes I know. And I am prouder of the fact that I haven't fought outside the ring than the fact that I have within it. Jiu Jitsu teaches you that you are not made of glass. You know what you are. Your Self was forged on the mats with every training session. And the stronger you become, the less concerned you are with whether others notice.

While on the Jocko podcast, Peterson said:

> "A good person is not a harmless person. He is a very dangerous person who has that under voluntary control."

He shares this sentiment in this chapter, when he says:

> "There is very little difference between the capacity for mayhem and destruction, integrated, and strength of character. This is one of the most difficult lessons of life."

Jiu Jitsu gives us the tools to harm others. Yet for most, the greater their skill, the more they look to contribute to, rather than take away from, their environment. Through countless hours of training, they have not just been training Jiu Jitsu: they have been training their souls. The Jiu Jitsu academy is an environment which removes your weakness out of necessity. There is simply no place for it.

Earlier in this chapter, Peterson cites nature as "that which selects." By its nature, Jiu Jitsu self-selects truly admirable human beings. Jiu Jitsu is difficult. You must fail daily. You must work with others. Delay gratification. Make sacrifices. Put forth great effort. You must pay attention and want to improve.

All of this leads to communities of truly exceptional individuals striving toward self-actualization. And when we do that, we don't just change ourselves, we change our world:

"Thus strengthened and emboldened, you may choose to embrace Being, and work for its furtherance and improvement."

Jiu Jitsu is the vehicle by which we improve the world, starting with ourselves. The modern world offers few avenues by which to purposefully cultivate such strength. Jiu Jitsu provides this environment, and in forging our strength, gives us the ability to use that strength in the service of others.

Peterson often says we are nodes in a network. Each of us will know 1000 people in our lives (at least). That means we are one person removed from 1 million people and two people removed from a billion.

Who we become shapes the world in ways we can never truly understand. We are connected to something far greater than ourselves and play a tangible and integral role in the betterment of Being. We owe it to ourselves, our neighbor, and the rest of humanity to be better. Jiu Jitsu helps us do that, by giving us the strength and confidence with which to stand up straight, with our shoulders back, and fight on behalf of the Good.

Rule 2

Treat Yourself Like Your Someone Responsible For Helping

Peterson opens the chapter with a surprise. Statistics show that people are more likely to fill and use prescriptions for their pets than themselves. The rest of the chapter is an attempt to understand why.

Treat yourself like someone you are responsible for helping. What does this mean in the context of Jiu Jitsu? I think it's this:

That our lives improve in proportion to our growth as martial artists. Sincere pursuit of understanding in grappling fosters a focus and competence on the mat that permeates into the rest of our experience. Everything is connected, and the advancement in one aspect of our being pulls along the whole of our being. We know this. So, to treat ourselves like someone we are responsible for helping, is to purposefully seek continued development in our technical progress in Jiu Jitsu.

Enter one of Peterson's most fundamental schemas:

> "These are the necessary elements whose interactions define drama and fiction. One of these is chaos. Another is order. The third (as there are three) is the process that mediates

between the two, which appears identical to what modern people call consciousness."

This is the tripartite structure of the hero's journey: the knower, the known, and the unknown. For our purposes, this is the practitioner, his or her areas of competence, and his or her areas of ignorance. And our ignorance always surpasses our knowledge. We each possess a few techniques and positions with which we have great skill. If you watch the high-level grapplers compete, though they are good at everything, they are truly great only at a few things. Thus, they seek to keep the competition in those realms to maximize victory. We have the same tendency. But it is this search for comfort that must be transcended.

How You Define Yourself Determines What You See

In heated moments of training with a peer, we tend to rely on our go-to techniques as we seek to maximize our chances of immediate success. Though our repertoire is vast, we generally attempt only a handful of techniques with someone whose skill we truly respect. This is how we succeed in the present moment. It is not, however, how we achieve our highest selves.

"...all the things we have come to know were born, originally, of the unknown..."

This is the Joseph Campbell idea that the cave you fear to enter holds the treasure that you seek. If we stay within our areas of competence, we will never transcend that competence. Our egos are bound to success in the immediate at a sacrifice of long term growth. There are always those teammates who never improve, no matter how long they stay on the mat. And it's because of the myopic thinking that believes success today means success in the final analysis. It's so easy to fall into this trap and seek the path of least resistance. When a guard pass works, it is not self-evident why we should avoid using it.

This choice comes down to a matter of identity and two entirely different modes of being: do we define ourselves as what we are or what we could be?

If you define yourself as what you are, you will strive to protect what you are. You cannot allow yourself to lose in the present moment because then you are less. So you wall yourself off. You practice only those techniques with which you anticipate success, and just like the movie *Groundhog Day*, you become a beast of routine. A beast which does not grow.

But when you define yourself by what you could be, when self-actualization is your highest goal, you have no need to defend what you are. Because you are not going to stay there for long. You don't want to be what you are. You want to be something more. You have no problem risking failure in the moment because the moment is not your concern. You will sacrifice immediate success in the hopes of a brighter tomorrow. You will risk losing the battle, because paradoxically, it's the only way to win the war.

The Way

Peterson references the mythological phoenix often. A symbol of resurrection, we are to embody the example of the phoenix as we constantly burn off suboptimal aspects of our being in place of new ones. He reminds his readers and listeners that our goal is not to be without flaws, but to be the being who continually realizes his flaws and overcomes them. The way to enact this mode of being is found in the symbolism of Taoism.

Most readers are familiar with the Taoist symbol of yin and yang -- the black paisley with the white dot and the white paisley with the black dot. Before Peterson, I saw this as a representation of the polarity of being -- the balance between light and dark, good and evil, masculine and feminine. But Peterson offered a different, more fundamental, interpretation: the two halves represent order and chaos, the known and the unknown; and the Tao, "the way," is the line that runs between them.

The optimal path of being is to walk the razor's edge between order and chaos. This parallels the Buddha's doctrine of the "middle way," and on this tightrope we find meaning:

"When life suddenly reveals itself as intense, gripping, and meaningful; when time passes and you're so engrossed in what you're doing you don't notice -- it is there and then that you are located precisely on the border between order and chaos."

This is where Jiu Jitsu is most exciting. Not when you are doing your favorite guard pass that you use fifty times a night with inevitable success. And not when you flail about aimlessly attempting a technique that far surpasses your competence. Jiu Jitsu is most exciting in the middle: when you are training with a peer whose skill forces you to venture just off the beaten path into areas of pseudo-competence. Where success is not guaranteed but, with complete concentration and commitment to the task at hand, is possible. It's when you have one foot in order, using your tool box, and the other in chaos, in the hopes of acquiring new tools.

This is the nature of skill acquisition. To constantly exceed yourself, bit by bit. To walk that fine line between order and chaos, known and unknown, as you push your boundaries to establish farther ones. And this takes courage. You must be willing to fail.

Peterson often references Jung's idea that the Joker is the precursor to the Savior: that you must be willing to be a fool before you can become a master. But few are willing to fulfill the necessary conditions that make this so. Our culture does not praise failure. And this success bias leads many people to quit Jiu Jitsu. We denigrate falling short while ignoring the fact that all success is preceded by consistent failure.

This is one of the reasons why Jiu Jitsu communities are such special places. It is a collection of people who are willing to fail so that they may become more. And if they are doing this on the mat, they are most likely doing this in their personal and professional lives as well.

We confront our shortcomings so that we may overcome them. We have no choice.

The Naked Truth

You cannot hide in Jiu Jitsu. It is one of the most honest experiences I have ever been a part of. If you are not training, it shows. If you are not staying in shape, it shows. And when you are fortunate enough to have high quality training partners, the areas of your game that you neglect show with pristine clarity.

In this chapter, Peterson references over-protective parents and their inability to protect their children from the problems of life:

> "It is far better to render Beings in your care competent than to protect them."

The same holds true for our weaknesses in grappling that we so often try to protect. If we are competent enough to control the outcome of a roll, we can be sure that the gameplay does not take place in our areas of discomfort. Or even more shamefully, we can simply not train with people who force us to go there. The choice stems from that fundamental problem of self-identity.

Someone who is concerned with what they are will avoid their weaknesses and the training partners who illuminate them to defend what they are. Someone concerned with what they are becoming will purposefully put themselves in those positions and seek out the training partners who force them to go into the unknown and acquire new skill.

Peterson asks:

"What does it mean to know yourself naked…"

It is an honest self-assessment of what you are. It is a close look at the tendencies you exhibit when you train and an analysis of the difficulties you encounter. To know one's self as naked is to admit your own shortcomings. To see beyond the belt on your waist, or your previous accolades, and hold yourself to a higher standard. It is to imagine what mastery would be and to acknowledge how far short you fall from that ideal.

"The Ideal shames us all."

But it also inspires us. Jiu Jitsu is infinite and so is our need for improvement in every position and technique. There are literally limitless ways in which you can improve, so that no matter who you are training with, each offers an opportunity for your advancement.

I had a conversation recently with parents who said they wanted their child to train with another student because that student presented the only challenge for their child's development. This is an archetypal misunderstanding I tried to rectify. I explained to them that it is not the responsibility of the training partner to challenge us, it is our responsibility to challenge ourselves. And the better we get the truer this becomes. We must practice "extreme ownership" and take full responsibility for our progress by using new techniques, on different sides, in different ways, to challenge ourselves.

There is always an opportunity to improve. And it is found in our willingness to confront the unknown, venturing into a little bit of chaos, so that we can construct new order.

> "But only you know the full range of your secret transgressions, insufficiencies and inadequacies. No one is more familiar than you with all the ways your mind and body are flawed."

You may have a great guard, but you play guard only on your right hip. You may be a smothering guard passer, but you pass only one way. You may have a great guillotine, but you don't know how to do a D'arce. We are all so terribly limited.

Our further progression is contingent upon our willingness to acknowledge the need for that progression. We cannot define success by the events of the roll. This is too short-sighted. Success is found in taking actions which lead to the manifestation of our highest selves in the future. This is a pact we must make with ourselves.

> "You must keep the promises you make to yourself, and reward yourself, so that you can trust and motivate yourself."

The Choice

The events of a roll easily tempt us off this path. We must know our purpose.

I always have a personal curriculum separate from the academy's focus. These are the techniques and tactics that I seek in live training and that make my training with less experienced teammates truly exciting. Sometimes this becomes a game within the game, as I strive to work on certain things without my partner knowing my focus. Other times for added difficulty, I handicap myself by explicitly telling my partner what I am looking for. This becomes the minigame within the game of Jiu Jitsu. But more importantly, it's part of the metagame of which Jiu Jitsu is a part.

My purpose for training is to continue to develop my understanding of Jiu Jitsu so that I come to better understand myself. When I grow in this discipline, my humanity improves, as my actions in the art are aiming at achieving my highest self in its totality, not solely in this discipline. This is the focus, but it is a focus that can easily become distorted.

Egos are strong. I have this focus, but the moment I get compromised training with a peer, I feel a strong urge to resort back to my areas of competence so that I can win the moment. I save face but lose myself. I missed out on an opportunity for some purposeful growth-inducing chaos because I overvalued the events of that roll.

This is where the definitiveness of purpose comes in. We must hold fast to our ideal. Defining ourselves by what we could be rather than what we are. We are willing to fail today so that we may succeed in the future. This is the best thing we can do for our technical progress within the art and is therefore the best thing we can do for our humanity.

This is how you treat yourself like you're someone responsible for helping.

Rule 3
Make Friends With People Who Want The Best For You

This is another one of those Petersonisms whose wisdom matches its simplicity. Of course we should surround ourselves with people who want the best for us. But these people are hard to find. Everyone has their own problems and responsibilities. It takes a special individual to see beyond their own subjective chaos with the genuine hope of helping you transcend your own.

This is what it means to be a friend. And with the help of Jordan Peterson and the New Testament, I have come to understand what friendship really means, and it begins with being a friend to yourself.

Love Your Neighbor

Having grown up in western society, most are familiar with the proclamation of Jesus:

> "Love your neighbor as yourself."- Mark 12:31

How am I supposed to do this? My only interaction with my neighbor is the occasional morning when we walk out to our cars at the same time. An exchange of pleasantries is the extent of our relationship. But I am my constant companion and know myself in a way I can never know another.

We are all so different with our unique experiences and dispositions. It's hard to love someone I don't really understand. It's hard enough to love one's self. But "love" is a term so commonplace that its meaning has become unclear. I tell my girlfriend I love her and with the next breath I say I love pizza. I use the same word to describe very different relationships, and the "love" in love your neighbor as yourself means something entirely different.

Radical acceptance of who I am is not true love. I don't show love by patting myself on the back when I fall short of my ideal or by lowering my standards to accept the day's performance.

I love myself by holding myself to a rigorous code of character: one of effort, attention, discipline, and compassion. I show love to myself by eating salads. Working out when I don't want to. Lying on the foam roller. Reading difficult books. By forcing myself to write when the blank page intimidates me.

I show love to myself by holding myself accountable to a worthy ideal. Love and self-discipline are synonymous, as I sacrifice the pleasures of the present moment for the difficult choices that lead to a better tomorrow. Self-love is not radical acceptance of what one is. Self-love is being disciplined so that we may become what we might be.

> "Assume first that you are doing the easiest
> things, and not the most difficult."

I am constantly surprised by the degree to which I lie to myself or rationalize sub-optimal behavior. I lead a disciplined life but constantly catch myself using my time in ways that will not further my aim. My potential is daily sacrificed to the insidious pleasures of modern living. Social media will rob me of the day if I am not on guard. And that extra cup of coffee will catch up to me in time.

We must be on constant guard against our weakness. And we can't do it alone. We need friends who will remind us when we fall short of our ideal. We must support each other's upward aim. This is what a true friend does. This is what it means to love your neighbor as yourself.

Love is to hold each other to our highest ideals, to further each other's aim, and to remind each other when we are headed in the wrong direction. This is the type of friend we must be for others.

This is how we must love each other, but not everyone is ready for this love.

The Downside of Aiming Up

Self-actualization is hard. It is a campaign of self-improvement that involves daily struggle. Since I discovered football at fifteen years old, I have spent most of my waking time sincerely pursuing a goal. Over the years, I have noticed a disconnect with many friends as a result.

I have sacrificed countless Friday and Saturday nights out with friends so that I could read, write, and train the next day. When I discovered the value of reading, I could no longer mindlessly watch television. Drinking with friends was no longer fulfilling. It was emptying. I wanted a better life. So, I had to live a better life.

Many times, I have had to change or abandon relationships because I saw that they were no longer serving me. They were comfortable for who I was, but they would not lead me to who I wanted to be. I could no longer sacrifice the future to stay in the present. I took time away from people I loved because I knew, together, we were not aiming up. You are the average of the people you spend the most time with. If your friends aren't showing love to themselves, they are unlikely to show it to you. They will pull you down by osmosis.

And they may not be aiming down. Sometimes they don't aim at all. They are content to be what they are and accept the lot they inherit. Working the jobs they dislike and getting together on weekends to numb the dissatisfaction with sports and alcohol. This is the common mode of being for the average late twenties/early thirties American. And there is an appeal there.

> "It's easier to put off until tomorrow what needs to be done today, and drown the upcoming months and years in today's cheap pleasures."

I cannot fault someone for avoiding the life of personal development. It's exhausting to daily sacrifice the pleasures of today for the joys of tomorrow. And it's easy for a group of friends to fall into passivity and because it is so ubiquitous, never question it. But we were meant for more.

We have a responsibility to our companions to strive toward our highest selves. To the degree that we do so, their lives will improve. To passively accept the prescription of the multitudes, and to bring others along with you, is not being a friend. A companion, sure. But not a friend. We are nodes in a network. Our choices affect the lives of those around us. It is our obligation to positively influence those around us, by holding ourselves and our companions to a high ideal that forces daily improvement and abstinence from that which does not serve us.

This is friendship.

A True Friend

A friend loves you as himself. A friend does not hand you another beer as you squander what you could become for what you currently are. He or she does not idly watch as you trade your potential for bad habits. A friend demands more of you. He requests your highest self and will not accept your downward aim.

"Friendship is a reciprocal arrangement."

I have had many companions over a lifetime, but by this definition of the word, few friends. For someone to love you as they love themselves, in a way which furthers your progress, implies that they must be doing the same for themselves: daily striving to remove their inefficiencies, cultivating new aspects of their being while striving to achieve more in the world. It is only those who are truly walking the path that can remind us when we step off it. And there is little traffic on this extra mile. When we find others who truly love themselves, and therefore can love us, we must cherish these relationships.

> "If you surround yourself with people who support your upward aim, they will not tolerate your cynicism and destructiveness. They will instead encourage you when you do good for yourself and others and punish you carefully when you do not."

The Purple Circle

I have mentioned these guys in every book I have written. These are true friends. My core group of teammates, the team within the team, with whom I pursued the same goal with equal fervor and discipline. It was this shared suffering which united us. We spent a good seven years training together nearly every day. Holding each other accountable. Teaching each other everything we knew. Honestly telling each other where we were strong and where we were weak. Explicitly communicating to one another how we could each be beaten to foster each other's growth as well as our own. We competed together. We fought together. And we lived together.

I have become the godfather of Pete McHugh's firstborn. I officiated Rob Cook's wedding. And I love Max Bohanon and Nick Liaskos like brothers.

I always wanted the best for them. I loved my neighbor as myself. And they returned the favor.

A good friend loves you but reminds you that you are not what you could be. And a great friend is the catalyst for your continued evolution. Throughout my journey in Jiu Jitsu, Pete McHugh has been such a friend.

He was my first teacher in the noon class on South Broad street. He was the one who encouraged me to compete as a white belt. It was his prodding that got me invited to the MMA team. With encouragement and tutelage, he taught me to teach. The example he set by opening his own school undoubtedly gave me the confidence to do the same. And his commitment to his beautiful wife played a big part in my leaving Stoic asceticism and pursuing a meaningful relationship.

This is what a friend is. He loves you for what you are but reminds you that you could be so much more. Often not even in words. Simply by living a life in which he loves himself and pursues constant improvement as he chases his own ideal, he implores you to do the same.

> "It is for this reason that every good example is a fateful challenge, and every hero, a judge. Michelangelo's great perfect marble David cries out to its observer: 'You could be more than you are.'"

This is a clear depiction of the mindset that runs through Peterson's book, the need to identify with what one could become rather than what one currently is. This is foundation of the Jiu Jitsu community.

The Community

> *Where we pursue individual goals as a collective.*

That is our academy's tagline and the only words written on our barren walls to remind our students of their common mission. And with it comes an implicit truth that is the heart of the Jiu Jitsu academy:

Everyone in the academy has a goal.

This is what makes the Jiu Jitsu environment so special. Each night, people from all walks of life come together to strive toward a better version of themselves. Some want to lose weight. Others want to learn a skill. Some want to test those skills in competition. But each of us sacrifices time and money and often health to suffer on the mats so that we may become more.

Our students and families consistently comment on our culture, praising our leadership for the community we have created. In truth, the culture is more a reflection of people who walk in the door than our efforts. Everyone is aiming toward something. Everyone is aiming up. And when we all do that together, magic happens. The culture is easy when everyone is living according to a worthy ideal.

This is the environment which allows for true friendship, in which we each love our neighbors as ourselves, holding each other accountable to our highest ideals, calling each other out when we miss class or take a round off.

We each want what is best for ourselves. And we each want what is best for each other. These two are mutually intertwined. Selfish altruism has its merits. When my teammates get better at Jiu Jitsu, I have better training partners and I will get better at Jiu Jitsu. If only for personal gain, it behooves me to support my teammate's development. But our motivations always transcend personal aims. The shared suffering of worthwhile struggle invariably helps us see beyond ourselves and into the heart of another.

The title of this chapter carries with it an implicit presupposition: those who want what's best for you must want what is best for themselves. True friends are striving toward their own goals, out of respect for themselves as well as the direct influence their progress will have on the quality of your life. And it is those who are making such sacrifices themselves who will understand the sacrifices your continued progress requires. This understanding is the prerequisite for support and encouragement.

Make friends with people who want the best for themselves. It is only they who can want what is truly best for you.

Rule 4
Compare Yourself To Who You Were Yesterday, Not To Who Someone Else Is Today

This is another one of those self-evident truths which is as hard to embody as it is easy to say. Peterson opens the chapter discussing the effect social media has had on our primordial counters that are always measuring where we stand within our competence hierarchies.

Before we were all so interconnected, you could be the best at a given trade in your town and enjoy the serotonin-based advantages of being atop that particular hierarchy. But as we become increasing connected, our hierarchies expand. It's getting harder and less likely to achieve that top position due to the expansion of our domain.

Our newsfeed is the conduit through which we receive the successes of others. We each broadcast our accomplishments, simultaneously raising the stakes within our field while lowering the esteem of others. The Jiu Jitsu community is hyper-active on social media. This is one of the reasons why our tribe has such strong ties. But this connection is also a great obstacle to our fulfillment, and social media is a tool we all use that no one truly understands.

A Modern Experiment

There are no rules on social media. We are each given a platform, with practically no restrictions, to use as we wish. We have no education in how to use it. This powerful tool for communication has become a conduit through which we express human weakness. Many have turned to using social media to seek attention, begging their followers for praise as they creatively strive to paint themselves in a certain light. It seems social media, like money, makes us more of what we already are.

If you are divisive and disagreeable, you engage in hostile debates. If you value education, you use this as a medium to share good ideas. But no matter your motivation, if you are not on watchful guard, you will easily slip into the trap of measuring your worth relative to the personas of those on your screen. And here is the cruel twist:

While you are on social media, you are at a personal low point. You are not engaging in something meaningful. You are either bored or avoiding something more important. You go to this well again and again and are never filled up. You are just biding your time until something better happens. And while you sit idly on your phone, you consume the often-fabricated highlights of other people's lives. You take in their best at your worst.

This is when that critical voice in your head pops up, telling you that you fall short. Our expanded network increases the size of our competence (notice the similarity to the word "competitive") hierarchies. No matter your accomplishments, every time you open a social media app, you are painfully reminded of all those more successful than you. And there are always those who, in one specific domain of life, have more than you do. Our mistake is to measure the total worth of our being through a single discipline. This is a natural and myopic reaction.

> "If the critical voice within says the same denigrating things about everyone, no matter how successful, how reliable can it be? Maybe its comments are chatter, not wisdom."

The Pie Chart

We each have a different aim constituted by varying values and positions in life. For the last decade, I have seen students measure their progress and worth relative to their classmates at the sacrifice of their own well-being. They compare the differences in their guard passing to one another without acknowledging the differences in their lives. A forty-something parent with a mortgage has a very different relationship to Jiu Jitsu than a twenty-year-old college kid living in his parents' basement. One can train twice a week, if they're lucky, while the other trains every day. One has an aged and injury-torn body with twice as many miles as the bullish ex-wrestler who's not old enough to drink. It's apples and oranges.

But we are quick to judge our worth, in our totality, compared to our peer group in a specific domain.

This is a great disservice to our progress and emotional health. We must have an honest self-assessment of what Jiu Jitsu is in the context of our lives: not relative to others but relative to our goals. The forty-something parent who wants to lose weight will have a very different relationship to training than the twenty-year-old who dreams of being a world champion.

Each must act according to his or her own values.

We must determine what Jiu Jitsu is to us. Who are we striving to become? We must know what type of training that better version of ourselves requires. Maybe we just want to lose weight and make some friends. Getting in twice a week, sweating and smiling, is sufficient for our goal. But if your goal is to be a world champion, you will sacrifice the rest of your life toward that aim: training multiple times a day, every day, with unrivaled intensity.

Without knowledge of your aim, your training is inefficient. When you know who you want to become, you know how to use Jiu Jitsu to help you get there. And with this knowledge you come to understand what type of Jiu Jitsu to play.

Your Game

> "To begin with, there is not just one game at
> which to succeed or fail. There are many games,
> and more specifically, many good games --
> games that match your talents... The world
> allows for many ways of Being. If you don't
> succeed at one, you can try another. You can
> pick something better matched to your unique
> mix of strengths, weaknesses and situation."

This is one of my favorite aspects of Jiu Jitsu. There is
no specific way in which Jiu Jitsu must be played. There
are myriad "games" to embody and you are free to play
Jiu Jitsu in a way which is optimal for your unique body
and temperament.

Big guys can play big guy games. Small guys can play
fast games. And each of us can learn to express the finer
aspects of our being through the way we practice, and
approach, this art. If you use this gift appropriately, Jiu
Jitsu becomes a mirror through which you come to
know yourself and a canvas through which you express
your deepest axioms on the human experience.

This is freedom.

Once you have acquired enough skill, you reach a point
when you start to remove aspects of your Jiu Jitsu to
find your game. You burn off all the deadwood and are
left with only the useful material. If deep half guard
doesn't work for you, you stop trying to play it. If you

46

find that your body naturally excels at a certain mode of passing, you build your game around that.

Every Jiu Jitsu player will inevitably cultivate his or her own game, it's just that few do so deliberately.

Pay attention to what gives you trouble. Pay attention to what comes easy. And learn to mold your game in accordance with your abilities, as you find the truest expression of yourself through this discipline.

> "You must decide what to let go and what to pursue."

And once you have a game, you must learn how to play this game with ever-increasing skill.

The Nature of Improvement

> "We cannot navigate without something to aim at and, while we are always in this world, we must always navigate... We are always and simultaneously at point "a" (which is less desirable than it could be), moving towards point "b" (which we deem better, in accordance with our explicit and implicit values)."

This schema of the unbearable present and the desired future, with the course of action that bridges this gap, is a fundamental lens through which to interpret the world and proves equally viable for Jiu Jitsu.

Example:

Professor passed my guard. It would be good if Professor did not pass my guard. That would mean I am improving. To prevent this, I must get better at grip fighting. And once better at grip fighting, I need to improve my ability to play guard on my left hip. By improving this weakness, I will be able to safely defend the position and not get my guard passed.

And as soon as we meet this desired future, we will set the stakes higher. Defending guard against Professor will become our new unbearable present as we seek to develop the ability to sweep from this position. We will practice a new course of routines and practices to bring this desired future into reality. We will repeat this process, ad infinitum.

Small Improvements

One of Peterson's major tenets is the power of small, incremental progress.

> "What could I do, that I would do, to make life a little better?"

This has become a maxim for me. I have asked myself this question every day since I read it and have never found a shortage of things to improve. From the stack of bills on my desk, to the clutter in the kitchen cabinets, there is always something that can be done that will improve the quality of my experience.

My life has grown less chaotic and more enjoyable as I truly ask this question and responded to its dictates. And my Jiu Jitsu has improved in proportion.

Consider the following example:

I want to get better at guillotines. What could I do, that I would do, to make my guillotines a little better? I could drive up to NYC to take a private lesson with Marcello Garcia. I could do this. But I won't. I cannot stand the crowdedness of the city and there are few goals that would bring me there. I recently opened my own school and have no money to pay for the tolls, let alone the private itself. Not to mention that the writing of this book is currently more meaningful than improving my guillotine.

I could drive to NYC for a private. But I won't. I would, however, watch a Marcello Garcia instructional video on YouTube. This is something I could do, that I would do, to improve my guillotine. This would make my Jiu Jitsu a little better.

If I did something like this every day, or even only once a week, my Jiu Jitsu would be much better than it is now.

There are always these small improvements to be made. And if we just ask that question, "What could I do, that

I would do, to make my Jiu Jitsu a little better?", our minds will become flooded with answers. Then we'd have an aim and actionable steps to help us achieve our goal.

"What you aim at determines what you see."

When you aim properly, you will find there are limitless ways to improve your grappling. Your eyes will become open to tools, to that which allows you to achieve your goal as you move from the unbearable present to the desired future. And these tools are everywhere. Maybe there are good videos on YouTube. Maybe one of your classmates knows something you don't and will be willing to share his or her experiences. Maybe there is a seminar nearby this weekend.

No matter your skill level, none of us has grown so much to render this question unanswerable. There is always more to be done. That is the beauty of an infinite ideal. It can never be reached and thus fills your life with perpetual meaning:

> "Perhaps happiness is to be found in the journey uphill, and not the fleeting sense of satisfaction awaiting at the next peak."

The Greatest Ideal -- Your Highest Self

Through Peterson I learned about Jung's idea of the Self, the aspect of your psyche which exists across personal transformations and informs your action by making things meaningful. This is a profound theory of personal development which seems almost self-evident.

> "You can use meaning to orient yourself in your life." - Jordan Peterson, *2017 Maps Of Meaning* lecture series

It is that Self that beckons you to be more than you are. But that Self could not care less what you are relative to another. You are playing your own game. The game of self-actualization in which you become something uniquely your own that no one else can be. And every moment is a chance to become someone who more closely resembles that highest self.

When we ask questions like, "What could I do, that I would do, to make my life [or Jiu Jitsu] a little better?" our Self will always be there to respond. This is what we use to guide our actions forward, not aiming at what others are, but at what only we can become.

And so, the accomplishments of others have no bearing on our present. We are not running a race against our contemporaries. We are racing against time to become what we are supposed to be. This progress can be measured only relative to who we were yesterday, and what someone else is today has nothing to do with this pursuit.

RULE 5
DO NOT LET YOUR CHILDREN DO ANYTHING THAT MAKES YOU DISLIKE THEM

Clearly this has nothing to do with your cultivation of skill in Jiu Jitsu. It does, however, provide a good framework for teaching kids. If you are not a parent or a kids instructor, this may be of little use to you. Feel free to skip this chapter. If you are, this is a powerful idea I learned from Peterson.

Peterson talks about the common mistake of parents who try to be their child's friend rather than parent. The role of the parent, certainly for the first four years, is to socialize the child so that they may make friends -- not to be one.

The same is true of the Jiu Jitsu instructor.

Jiu Jitsu is a vehicle through which children learn socialization, discipline, effort, and delayed gratification. The child's time spent on the mat is basic training for life. As instructors, we are to use the opportunities that Jiu Jitsu presents to give our students the tools to lead meaningful and productive lives. We are not training for sport. We are training for life. And to do this properly, we need to be a child's mentor rather than a friend.

A thought:

As discussed in Rule 3, a true friend holds you to a high ideal and calls forth your best as they support your attainment of your highest self. This is performed in love. This is how we show love to our students. Not with radical acceptance and free-wheeling fun, but by placing purposeful constraints on these kids so that they may blossom into something more. That is true friendship. And in this sense, I am honored to be the friend of each of my young students.

Having a Good Class

For these students to use Jiu Jitsu as a vehicle for personal development, they need to have good classes: being focused during instruction, performing the techniques well, and taking care of their partners while they put forth great effort. For many young students, this is a lot to ask of them at first, so we start small and consistently reward good behavior no matter how seemingly irrelevant. This is not a new idea.

Peterson references B.F. Skinner, the behavior psychologist who taught pigeons to play ping pong, a seemingly impossible task:

> "Skinner observed the animals he was training to perform such acts with exceptional care. Any actions that approximated what he was aiming

at were immediately followed by a reward of just the right size: not small enough to be inconsequential, and not so large that it devalued future rewards."

In the academy, we call this *catch them doing something right*.

Let's say little Johnnie has trouble paying attention. Whenever I catch him focusing, I will go out of my way to praise him in front of his peers. Something as simple as "I love how Johnnie is sitting seiza" will bring a smile to his face and increase the likelihood of Johnnie repeating this behavior in the future.

Over the years I have seen so many troubled students become model citizens on the mat, simply by repeatedly and publicly acknowledging them when they perform a behavior we ask of them.

There are many components to having a good class, the macro routine of "good class" is broken up into many micro-routines: having a good warm-up, being focused during instruction, practicing good technique, taking care of their partners, putting forth effort. Some kids just get it and can do all of these on their first day. With others it takes time, and you focus on one micro routine at a time, as you slowly build their ability to have a good class.

And as you do, just like the good friend in Rule #3, you hold them to an increasingly higher standard that is clearly communicated. You let them know that you see what they can become, and that your job is to help them get there.

Socialization

Our individual goals should be aligned with our society, as our higher aim brings the whole world with us. Our pursuit of personal development is most useful when it acts on behalf of Being, bringing more Good into the world than could have been had without us. And so our efforts, even in private, have a social component which exceeds ourselves.

If we are to change the world, we must learn how to work with the world, with others. This is the environment Jiu Jitsu provides due to the structure of class and the nature of the art, and it's invaluable:

> "...peers are the primary source of socialization after the age of four. Rejected children cease to develop, because they are alienated from their peers. They fall further and further behind, as the other children continue to progress. Thus, the friendless child too often becomes the lonely, antisocial or depressed teenager and adult."

We cannot do Jiu Jitsu alone. A good class requires cooperation with your partner: physically, as we must give a specific reaction to be a good uke; mentally, as partners engage in group problem-solving as they seek to understand the complexities of the art; and emotionally, as the nature of dominant positions teaches us empathy as we attend to the feelings of our partners while they are in compromised positions.

We daily stress the importance of not hurting your partners. Jiu Jitsu is an empathic art. The student must understand how their partner is feeling, whether it's focusing on their fatigue to win a scramble or their pain to safely protect them from injuries. When we do this, we are training ourselves to focus on how others are feeling and transcend the subjective nature of our experience. Children who learn to attend to the well-being of their partners will carry this skill into adulthood, becoming better parents, employees, and friends in the process.

Individuality

By running a tight ship as an instructor, I have often worried I was limiting these kids in the expression of their individuality. We are organized with our classes. All kids wear the same uniform. They sit in a line quietly. They are told when to stand and when to move. There is an authoritarian aspect to it. Peterson, and Nietzsche through him, have helped me better understand the need for this structure:

> "It is the primary duty of parents to make their children socially desirable. That will provide the

> child with opportunity, self-regard, and security. It's more important even than fostering individual identity. That Holy Grail can only be pursued, in any case, after a high degree of sophistication has been established."

This was Nietzsche's idea that you had to be a slave before you could be free, that we need a discipline to mold our humanity, honing our abilities as we remove the superfluous so that we become truly capable of pursuing a vision uniquely our own. This is the role society plays. Society comes with many restrictions but serves as the bedrock we stand upon as we pursue our highest selves.

It simultaneously restricts and upholds the individual. This is what a good Jiu Jitsu academy does.

We use Jiu Jitsu as a vehicle to mold our young student's character. We set high expectations which greatly limit choices in the immediate. Our young students learn to focus, try, work with others, and to delay gratification; all the skills they will need to have a meaningful life in the future. Peterson states this beautifully in the final paragraph of the chapter:

> "A child who pays attention instead of drifting, and can play, and does not whine, is comical, but not annoying and is trustworthy--that child will have friends wherever he goes. His teachers will like him, and so will his parents. If he attends politely to adults, he will be attended to,

smiled at and happily instructed. He will thrive, in what can so easily be a cold, unforgiving and hostile world. Clear rules make for secure children and calm, rational parents. Clear principles of discipline and punishment balance mercy and justice so that social development and psychological maturity can be optimally promoted. Clear rules and proper discipline help the child, and the family, and the society, establish, maintain and expand the order that is all that protects us from chaos and the terrors of the underworld, where everything is uncertain, anxiety-provoking, hopeless and depressing. There are no greater gifts that a committed and courageous parent can bestow."

This is the value of our profession as Jiu Jitsu instructors. And this holds true for anyone who works with children. It is our responsibility to see that they are prepared to have a meaningful life that improves the world around them. We do this by constantly rewarding their behaviors that are aligned with this purpose, by addressing the micro routines that make up the big picture, and with patience, slowly encourage their continued evolution. That way when these kids grow up, they will have the tools to work with others and bring Good into the world. In so doing, they will find their highest selves and express their unique individuality.

This is our task and it is a noble one. Do not let your students do anything that makes you dislike them. Instead, give them a worthwhile challenge and praise their noble pursuit.

RULE 6
SET YOUR HOUSE IN PERFECT ORDER
BEFORE YOU CRITICIZE THE WORLD

In this, the shortest chapter in the book, Peterson discusses some of the darkest aspects of humanity: school shooters, serial killers, and the Gulags of Soviet Russia. With the former two, he shows how people can become so discontented with Being that they perceive the suffering inherent of life unworthy of life itself. In the latter, he shows how a single individual took the shortcomings of his situation and used it as a vehicle for deep introspection and self-improvement.

The title of the chapter is reminiscent of the words of Jesus:

> "And why beholdest thou the mote that is in thy brother's eye, but considerest not the beam that is in thine own eye?"- Matthew 7:2

And this where our grappling fruit is to be found.

Extreme Ownership

Most Jiu Jitsu readers are familiar with Jocko Willink. Retired Navy Seal and Brazilian Jiu Jitsu black belt, he has become the discipline spirit animal for many of us. With his daily 4:30 am Instagram posts and widely-consumed podcast on the lessons from a life of discipline, he advocates for extreme ownership: taking full responsibility for everything one encounters, thus rendering the individual capable of altering their experience. This is the fundamental freedom of the human experience which Viktor Frankl discussed in *Man's Search for Meaning*:

> "Everything can be taken from a man but one thing: the last of human freedoms -- to choose one's attitude in any given set of circumstances, to choose one's own way."

This is the freedom of conscious experience. And it is discipline that leads to this freedom.

In Rule 2, I mentioned a conversation with parents who said they wanted their child to train with another student because that student presented the only challenge for their child's development. This is the opposite of extreme ownership and could not be further from the mindset which seeks to set one's house in perfect order before criticizing the world.

A lesson I've learned from Peterson is that when you define something, you are also defining yourself. To suggest that no one can offer a challenge is to suggest that one cannot create challenges themselves.

The Responsibility Of The Individual

As you progress through this art, you will spend more time training with students less experienced than you. To keep progressing, it is your responsibility to use these individuals as tools for your personal development.

So many students continue to practice the same techniques that they are highly competent at. The continual success they find is ultimately to their detriment. If you are not struggling, you are not growing. It is the responsibility of the individual to create struggle when their partner cannot provide it.

As we've already discussed, each of us is far too limited to have exhausted our ability to grow while training with any partner. We each have our own tendencies and pockets of ignorance that we avoid. When training with a peer, we may stay in our areas of competence as we seek to win the exchange. Fine. But when training with a less experienced partner, you could always win those exchanges, which means they are not really wins; they are a purgatory. We must practice different techniques, ones in which we are not strong, to create struggle and facilitate progress.

There are nearly limitless ways to do this. You always pass right? Pass left. You play guard on your left hip? Get on the right. Etc. Etc.

If you always rely on your training partners to create the resistance your growth requires, you will soon stop growing. It is not their responsibility to make you grow. That rests on your shoulders. And as you progress, you are going to find fewer and fewer training partners who can challenge your best techniques. You must humble yourself, risk failure, and go to places where you are not strong so that you may acquire new strength. Like the phoenix, you must burn off feathers to be renewed. This is painful. But it's worth it. And no one can do it for you but yourself.

Alexander Solzhenitsyn survived the Gulags of Soviet Russia and wrote a detailed account of its horrors. He realized that the health of a society was contingent upon the integrity of the individual. That he, as well as all his countrymen, had contributed to the devastation of their nation by their own moral shortcomings. When he was in these concentration camps, he asked himself, and truly asked, what he had done wrong in his life to arrive at this point. He made an honest self-assessment of his own faults and understood how they contributed to the degradation of his state.

This is extreme ownership.

> "He took himself apart, piece by piece, let what was unnecessary and harmful die, and resurrected himself."

We must do the same with our Jiu Jitsu. If you think that you cannot get better training with someone, anyone, then your ego is far too big and your understanding of Jiu Jitsu too small. When we claim that others cannot challenge us, we are criticizing the world. We are selling ourselves, and our ability to strive toward our potential, short. We show a blanket ignorance of our understanding of Jiu Jitsu. There is perhaps no faster path to stagnation.

We are confined to the hours that we can train. None of us has enough mat time to truly understand every position and technique in Jiu Jitsu. And the deeper we get, the more there is to be seen. It's infinite. We must always ask:

> "Have you taken full advantage of the opportunities offered to you?"

And the answer is always no. My time in this art has made me painfully aware of my own ignorance and shortcomings. When training with a peer, there are only a handful of techniques that I use with extreme confidence. We all possess some techniques of extreme proficiency, few of us possess many, but none of us is this skilled with all of them. When training with the less experienced students, our job is to use these rounds as a laboratory: making experiments, forcing ourselves into chaos to construct habitable technique. We then take that understanding and apply it to an experienced grappler to check in on our growth. This is one of the best uses of your time in grappling. You may soon run out of teammates who challenge your best game. It is your responsibility to formulate new ones.

None of us is what we could be. Our potential beckons us forth. Mastery is an infinite ideal that will forever recede as we advance. We will never set our house in perfect order. There is just too much to be done.

Rule 7 to be discussed as the final chapter, for reasons to be explained.

RULE 8
TELL THE TRUTH,
OR AT LEAST, DON'T LIE

Peterson has taught that the western world is predicated on the Christian notion of true speech, the freedom with which we articulate our meandering thoughts to come to sound conclusions about our relationship to experience, using these findings to revivify the dead culture we inherit. This is what the mythological motif of rescuing the father from the belly of the whale represents. This notion of true speech comes in many forms, and at its foundation, we must be true to ourselves.

Tell Yourself the Truth

> "I rid myself, to the bottom of my soul, of primate-dominance motivations and moral superiority."

With this single sentence, Peterson describes the greatest obstacles to the development of both white and black belts. Humans have a complex biology governed by simple desires. As a white belt, what attracts so many to Jiu Jitsu are the motivations of primate dominance: we express our will over another's, demonstrating power in a safe and controlled environment. It is the addiction to this expression which often impedes learning.

The black belt's obstacle, however, is often entirely different. In being able to safely subdue most would-be assailants, his greatest adversary is often himself. Having achieved the top of this competence hierarchy, he is at the mercy of his morals. The trap which impedes technical development, and spiritual development, is a feeling of superiority. When you keep score relative to others, there is no motivation to keep ascending once you're ahead. Your past growth becomes the obstacle to further development.

This superiority on the mat can bleed into daily life, even where being a black belt in Jiu Jitsu has no direct merit in daily experience. I have a friend who tells everyone he meets, such as gas station attendants and waitresses, that he is a black belt, and expects to receive discounts due to his achievements in a completely unrelated discipline. Conversely, my friend and highly accomplished grappler Garry Tonon summed up the opposite stance nicely in a recent social media post:

> "I always find it funny when people are surprised when pro athletes f'up in other parts of life. Uh, yeah, I spent my whole life trying to get really good at one thing... The rest of my life is in shambles. Lol what do you expect? I'm not a God, lunatics, I'm good at a sport."

This is telling the truth. We must admit the simplicity of our biology if we have any hopes of overcoming it, keeping a watchful eye on our ego to be sure it doesn't go unchecked. No matter your experience level, you are always the greatest obstacle to your own development. This development continues when we are transparent not only to ourselves, but to others.

Tell Others The Truth

Our instructors and fellow students will not tell us what we pretend to know. We must have the humility to admit what we do not understand and the willingness to listen to what others have to say. Everyone on the mat knows something we don't. Each possesses a skill that could improve our ability to perform this art.

> "If you will not reveal yourself to others, you cannot reveal yourself to yourself. That does not only mean that you suppress who you are, although it means also that. It means so much of what you could be will never be forced by necessity to come forward."

Again, this theme of who we are vs. who we could be comes forth.

If we define ourselves by what we currently are, we will feel the need to defend that self. By defining myself as a "knowledgeable Jiu Jitsu practitioner," I possess the need to appear knowledgeable, and thus am less inclined to seek counsel for something I don't understand. But if I define myself as a "growing Jiu

Jitsu practitioner," I will embody the spirit of knowledge acquisition rather than the previous stance of knowledge defense. I will take part in the uncovering of knowledge, which is always taking place in areas yet explored -- often in the minds of others.

> "You can use words to manipulate the world into delivering what you want."

If we simply ask questions, and ask them properly, we have access to the experiences of other grapplers. When I ask Professor Almeida a question, his answer is based on twenty-some years of experience. I can learn from his experiences to allow me to save time in trial and error and stand atop his shoulders in hopes of seeing more than I currently do.

When we speak clearly and tell the truth, the world and our instructors will deliver what we seek.

Tell Yourself The Truth During Training

When we pursue mastery, we aim at an infinite ideal. No matter how well we grapple, there is always something we could have done better. Sometimes pride masks this truth.

> "The prideful, rational mind, comfortable with its certainty, enamored of its own brilliance, is easily tempted to ignore error, and to sweep dirt under the rug."

One of the greatest lessons I learned from Professor Almeida came due to his absence. When he was doing a lot of work with Gracie Barra in California, I was doing all my training with my teammates. I would be doing well, achieving positional advancements and submissions with what felt like great technique. But then he'd return, and a round with Professor would make me feel like a white belt. I couldn't understand it: I would go from feeling like I was well on my way to mastery and then, moments later, feel like a fool. I asked Professor to explain this disparity and he gave me this pearl of wisdom: train with others as if they were me.

This completely changed my game. I began to only practice techniques that would work on the world's best. And if I achieved any success in training, I only recognized such actions as progress if they would have worked on a Professor. If it didn't, it didn't count. I quickly saw how many of the techniques and tactics I was relying on in training were garbage when compared to what was required to achieve success against a truly high-level grappler.

I stopped ignoring my errors. I no longer swept dirt under the rug. And my Jiu Jitsu improved to the degree that I did. And when I failed, I didn't make excuses. I didn't blame my injuries or give credit to the abundant skill of a training partner. I simply told myself:

"I still have something to learn."

This theme echoes through Jordan Peterson's work and is prevalent in *12 Rules*. We are not what we could be. A better self beckons us forth, and the only way to move forward is in truth.

> "It is for this reason that Nietzsche said that a man's worth is how much truth he could tolerate. You are by no means only what you already know. You are also all that which you could know, if only you would. Thus, you should never sacrifice what you could be for what you are. You should never give up the better that resides within for the security you already have."

By identifying with what you could be and making that your goal, you create a relationship to the world that is always seeking your betterment. We are goal-directed creatures. We pursue our environment relative to that goal. When our goal is to improve in Jiu Jitsu, we no longer blind ourselves to that which makes this improvement possible. We seek out teachers. We pay attention. And sometimes the greatest teacher is ourselves.

We have a conscience which informs us when our actions are in accordance with our being. We possess something similar in Jiu Jitsu. Once we have a foundation of knowledge from our experiences in training, we know what good Jiu Jitsu feels like. We also know what bad Jiu Jitsu feels like. When I perform a sloppy technique relying too much on physicality, I feel dirty. I feel like I cheated on Jiu Jitsu. I feel like I have missed the mark.

> "If you pay attention to what you do and say, you can learn to feel a state of internal division and weakness when you are misbehaving and misspeaking."

That internal division and weakness is what it feels like to do Jiu Jitsu sub-optimally. The best practitioners I know are the hardest on themselves. This is because they are highly attuned to this feeling of internal division which arises when their movements are incongruent with the prescription of the situation. If we are truthful with ourselves during training, we will feel this often.

But it's so easy to achieve a sweep and feel good about yourself. To submit a partner and feel as though you achieved some final victory. To confuse success in the immediate with success in the final analysis. This is too myopic. And we do it too often.

Peterson taught me that Carl Jung believed that everyone acted out a myth, but few realized they were doing so. And that we had better know what myth we are acting out, because ours might be a tragedy.

What myth are you acting out in your Jiu Jitsu journey? Are you the exploratory hero who constantly confronts the unknown to acquire new skills? Or are you the tyrant, walling yourself off in safe space, never venturing away from your competence, protecting what you are while simultaneously preventing what you could be?

As Peterson puts it, are you:

> "Taking the easy way out or telling the truth -- those are not merely two different choices. They are different pathways through life. They are utterly different ways of existing."

I choose the way of the hero. I choose the way of admitting my own ignorance with the aim of becoming better. I choose to tell the truth, or at least, not to lie.

Rule 9
Assume That The Person You Are Listening To Might Know Something That You Don't

Peterson often reference's Jung's idea that everyone is the unconscious exponent of a dead philosopher. Human beings are vessels for ideas and we act them out, or more appropriately, they act us out.

G.K. Chesterton, the Christian writer and poet, told a story about his relationship to the Christian faith. He likened himself to a sailor, who set out to find the new world, and after an arduous odyssey, reached land only to realize that he had arrived on the shores of England from where he started. Chesterton's faith was no different. He set out to create a moral doctrine for Being and found that it had already been done two thousand years before.

> "Longest way round is the shortest way home."
> - James Joyce

My journey has been similar. I have spent my life exploring the humanities in search of answers, only to find that once I reconciled myself to those answers, I had achieved nothing new at all. I came to a healthy respect for the shortcomings of my own mind, and it was Peterson who helped me understand just how difficult true thinking is:

"People think they think, but it's not true. It's mostly self-criticism that passes for thinking. True thinking is rare -- just like true listening. Thinking is listening to yourself. It's difficult. To think, you have to be at least two people at the same time. Then you have to let those people disagree."

I had never heard thinking described like this. It makes sense. To think, you ask a question and then wait for yourself to respond. You volley back and forth between ideas until you form a conclusion. This takes a great deal of mental horsepower, and often in areas in which we possess a great deal of ignorance, true thinking proves too difficult to embody. So, we have conversations.

Conversations

Everyone on the mat knows something we do not. The more diverse your peer group, the more this proves to be the case. Different schools represent different ideologies, different modes of grappling, and with each comes a unique understanding specific to that school of thought.

Even within our own association, different styles of gameplay have been created despite us all learning from Professor Almeida. Out of Tom Deblass's school came Garry Tonon and Gordon Ryan with their emphasis on leg locks. From Professor Bongiorno comes the most technical sport guard work that you'll ever see. And all my students are embodying the principles of tight guard passing and top pressure. We each have chosen to focus on different aspects of Jiu Jitsu, and therefore, each possess a unique lens.

In Rule 4, we discussed my dear friend Pete McHugh. He recently taught a seminar at my school, focusing on guillotines and butterfly guard. I have a pretty good guillotine and have been focusing on it for the past few months. I paid close attention to the specifics of Pete's teaching and was shocked.

We had both learned the guillotine from one of the best, Ricardo Almeida, and here was my best friend, whose school is twenty miles down the road, teaching the guillotine in a way completely different from how I teach it. I was shocked at the disparity in our approach.

As I observed Pete instructing, my weaker nature made itself known as a slew of thoughts ran through my head:

That's not how you finish a good guillotine. That's not as good as my way. That's wrong.

I felt myself defending what I was and quickly writing off his approach. But then something greater inside me spoke up:

Maybe Pete knows something you don't. Man, his uke taps real fast with barely any squeeze. Maybe my way is wrong. He knows something I don't.

All of this flashed through my mind in mere moments, but it brought to light a fundamental choice. The choice we have continued to describe in this book:

Did I define myself by what I was or what I could be?

As soon as Pete finished teaching, I pulled him aside and picked his brain. I had to understand why he performed the guillotine the way he did and learn what he had to teach. There we stood, conversing about the guillotine. The kind of conversation I had been having with myself the past few months, but without his alternative experience to rely on. I learned about the fundamental difference of where our squeezes came from: mine from my arms and core, his from his hips. I became aware of a whole new aspect of the guillotine that I had never truly appreciated. And I came to this understanding through a conversation.

Search For Truth

> "A conversation such as this is one where it is the desire for truth itself -- on the part of both participants -- that is truly listening and speaking."

Far too often we engage in conversations just waiting for our chance to speak, trying to prove the worth of our opinion, defending that opinion rather than truly hearing what someone else has to say. Jiu Jitsu and the ego are forever bound. When we achieve success and define ourselves relative to our standing in the art, we are quick to wall ourselves off and attempt to justify our self-imposed limitations by assuming we have a definite answer. But Jiu Jitsu is subjective. It is performed differently with each body type on each body type. No matter how often you share the mat, your training partners will cultivate a very different understanding of a technique than you will.

If we are truly to use these training partners to our advantage, we must seek to understand their perspective. Then it will enrich our own. A good conversation is when two people come together to answer a question. They don't seek to justify their opinion; they seek truth. And truth is a cooperative effort.

Some of our best progress will come after training, while we are cleaning the mats and discussing random thoughts on grappling, when suddenly a teammate says something that we don't understand. We stop the conversation, and with genuine interest seek to better understand their position -- often revealing a world that we were unable to see unassisted.

This rule of assuming the person you are listening to might know something you don't is universal. It's easy to embody when you are talking to an instructor or someone with a higher rank than you. Sometimes it is harder with a peer, as that primate need to be atop the dominance hierarchy limits your ability to see the perspective of others because you are too busy defending your own.

We must swallow our pride and remember that truth, not personal identification, is our ultimate goal.

Everyone knows something we don't, and those who grow the most remember this truth. Have conversations. Listen to others. And allow their experience to inform your own. Every conversation is an opportunity to be more than you might have been.

Rule 10
Be Precise In Your Speech

Peterson has taught that we experience the world as a forum for action. Action requires a set of values, for there must be some criteria that makes one action more favorable than another. These values are expressions of your aim, your goal. Therefore, your aim provides the lens through which you interpret experience as the world manifests itself in three ways: tools, obstacles, and irrelevancies.

This simple codification of experience has helped me see the world, and my life, with increased clarity. We do not see objects. We see functions. When I see a chair, I see a place to sit before I see "chair." When I'm thirsty, a glass reveals itself as a vessel with which to acquire water before I recognize it as "glass."

Our goal determines what we see. Therefore, we had better make sure we have a clearly defined goal that reflects our truest aim. We must use precise speech. It is this clarity that will construe the world into habitable order, with clearly defined values of experience and objects. Without this singularity of focus, we stumble.

> "Why remain vague, when it renders life stagnant and murky?"

You cannot not have a goal. We all aim at something. But without a clearly defined goal, we cannot codify the world into tools, obstacles, and that which does not matter. We have no idea what matters. We invariably ignore tools that would assist us on our path and seek out obstacles which impede it. Just as detrimental, we are not afforded the ability to label things as irrelevant -- because we don't know what's irrelevant -- so we must entertain every aspect of experience in search for usefulness. This is inefficient, exhausting, and impractical.

The more clearly we define the goal, the more clearly opportunities for its achievement shine before us.

Acting According To Your Goal

I have had many Jiu Jitsu goals in my life. For years, my sole aim was to develop as much skill as possible. I wanted to "master" the art, and so I viewed my experience through the lens of this goal.

I built relationships with the best practitioners on our team, forging deep bonds rooted in reciprocity of skill acquisition. I competed. Not because I liked competing, but because it would force me to constantly seek my best self and create a singularity of attention in the months leading up to a tournament. I watched film to see how the best practiced this art and did my best to mimic them in training. I remember driving two hours into the city to be Professor Almeida's uke for a seminar, just to be able to feel what he was doing and observe his teaching style. I shaped my life around my goal, finding the tools that would help me achieve my vision. In so doing, I become aware of the obstacles which impeded its fulfillment.

I stopped going to the bar on Friday and Saturday nights. A good morning of training was worth more than any late night with friends. I started eating better, as junk food was no longer pleasure but pain that presented itself during training. And because the mastery of this art was all that mattered, I forwent intimate relationships. Having a girlfriend simply did not help my guard passing.

It was only years later that my aim changed as I sought a complete, holistic life. Had my goal never changed, neither would have my social life, and I would have missed out on the greatest aspects of the human experience. The goal that served my twenties would have robbed me of a good life in my thirties. We must constantly reassess our goals to ensure they are leading us to a place we want to go, and for many of us, that place is everchanging.

I'm 32 and no longer compete. I own a martial arts school and am focused on growing a community of like-minded people who strive for the betterment of the group. This community forces me to grow in all the ways I most need so that I may someday become the servant I envision. It's nice to be a white belt again.

My health now matters more than my technical development. I am no longer willing to accept the constant pain that comes from years of injuries. I now train with less volume, only practicing techniques that do not put unnecessary strain on my body; the leg entanglements and inverted attacks I loved so much are now a memory of the past. I use them infrequently, and my health has improved as a result. I find myself training slower and more methodically, avoiding the flashy techniques and staying in safe harbors of less kinetic energy, while truly *playing* Jiu Jitsu.

My primary goal is to use Jiu Jitsu as a vehicle for personal development as I build a community and improve the lives of our members. This is a different aim than focusing solely on my personal mastery, and my daily actions are representative of this change.

Your Goal Shapes Your Experience

Your aim determines what you see. During a class, there are twenty-some people on the mat who represent myriad relationships to Jiu Jitsu: some seek mastery, some want to compete, others want to become a teacher, most want to lose weight while others seek fellowship. Each of these goals creates a fundamentally different perspective.

With skill acquisition as the focus, the student tries to direct the roll toward one specific aspect of grappling and get as many reps as possible with one technique. While competing, the student will train as if it were a competition, with intensity and focus and the

84

scoreboard in mind, seeking to win the round. A student focused on becoming a teacher, however, will spend their rounds focused on his or her training partners, giving them constructive feedback to help them better understand the art.

A student using Jiu Jitsu to lose weight will concern his or herself with the metrics of heart rate and sweat, constantly moving to get a great workout. But if the student yearns for community, he or she will be happy simply engaging in a positive activity with a friend, enjoying the fellowship of the roll.

Jiu Jitsu is still Jiu Jitsu, but these varying goals dramatically shape the way we experience the art. If we are to use Jiu Jitsu as a vehicle for personal development, we must know how we wish to develop. Having a clearly defined goal that is aligned with our life's purpose allows us to use Jiu Jitsu in ways unique and optimal for our own being. To do anything else is to miss the opportunity of a lifetime which Jiu Jitsu presents.

Once you formulate a clearly defined goal, it is your responsibility to defend it.

Defend Your Goal

"Don't ever underestimate the destructive power of sins of omission."

My goal is to use Jiu Jitsu to build a community of fellowship and growth. There is nothing more vital to the community than the culture, so I defend our culture like it's my child. I have found great value in Mayor Giuliani's broken window policy, in which he lowered New York City's crime rates by killing the monster when it's small. He saw that dilapidated buildings welcomed graffiti, which encouraged loitering, which led to drug deals, violence, and death. The broken windows were the first chink in the armor which led to this snowball effect. He fixed the windows and the crime decreased.

It is the seemingly innocuous which lead to our destruction.

We have embodied this principle in our academy. We always bow on and off the mat. Black belt instructors are to be addressed as "Professor" and assistant instructors as "Coach." If a belt comes off while drilling, you take the time to retie it. Before each round of live training, you make yourself presentable to others while facing away from them. There is no cursing. And you get changed in the locker room.

All these subtle "rules" help prevent the obstacles from arising which are antithetical to our culture. Were I to ignore these things and let them slide, I would be contributing, by omission, to the degradation of the school.

The choice of inaction is itself an action contrary to my aim.

These subtle, daily conflicts are contrary to my nature. I am highly agreeable and do not welcome confrontation. But my goal to use Jiu Jitsu as a vehicle for personal development, to improve the lives of as many people as possible in Florence, NJ, far outweighs the discomfort of standing up for my values.

> "What if she [you] had continually and honestly risked conflict in the present, in the service of longer-term truth and peace?"

We must be willing to defend our purpose. And this holds true regardless of your goal. If your goal is to acquire as much skill as possible, then you need a peer group to do it. You need training partners that will challenge you and force your continued evolution. When you see those around you slacking, it is your responsibility to yourself to get them back on track.

A few years ago, the Tuesday and Thursday morning Jiu Jitsu practice had nearly disappeared. We had our pro team sparring, but none of the Jiu Jitsu guys were coming to train any more. I had, like the lonely kid on the playground, no one to play with! I could have just accepted it, chalking it up to circumstance, but that would have been a sin of omission. Instead, I practiced extreme ownership, personally texting each potential training partner every Monday and Wednesday night.

This action inevitably built the attendance back up and my quality training resumed.

I loved these guys and wanted to see them grow, but my primary motivation was self-centered. I needed training partners and would do whatever it took to acquire them. Sometimes this meant approaching a teammate and questioning his actions, reminding him that his actions were not representative of his words. This is hard, especially with a friend, but it was necessary. And we were all better off because of it.

Be Precise In Your Speech

> "Courageous and truthful words will render your reality simply, pristine, well-defined and habitable."

By clearly defining the goal, the world and its infinite variables becomes discernible. And a clearly defined goal removes much superfluous thinking. You know what is a tool and what is an obstacle. You know what doesn't matter. By having this clarity, we can act efficiently in the world toward our unique aim. We are given a chance to truly pursue self-actualization, because we have finally defined what that Self is that we wish to actualize.

By using precise speech, with ourselves and those around us, we find our path. And by using precise speech, with ourselves and those around us, we find the tools to stay on the path.

Rule 11
Do not bother kids when they are skateboarding

Peterson used to watch the kids skateboarding on campus. Admiring their fearlessness, he would marvel at their willingness to risk safety in pursuit of competency. He recognized the heroic nature of the discipline. But few did. Soon there were "skatestoppers" on any skateable edge. They were ugly, and worse, they impeded the kid's ability for adventure. He recalls seeing something similar when Toronto removed all school playgrounds with concerns for insurability, leaving kids either fending off boredom while playing in the dirt or running around on the roof of the school with excitement.

> "...when playgrounds are made too safe, kids either stop playing in them or start playing in unattended ways. Kids need playgrounds dangerous enough to remain challenging."

This is the playground Jiu Jitsu provides.

Children are little balls of kinetic energy. Their motors are ceaseless in a way we adults can faintly remember. This energy must be used. It will be used, and pending the vehicle, wonderful or disastrous effects will follow. Jiu Jitsu is the vehicle with which children can expend this bursting energy toward a worthwhile aim within the security of an organized community.

"Fight Nice"

My brother and I fought constantly growing up. My grandmom's commentary was simple: "Fight nice." This made no sense when I was eleven years old. Two decades later, her words echo with profundity.

This is what live training is. It's the outlet through which children can release those biological urges to physically control another in an organized setting with teammates who add the resistance which requires great effort. It is this expenditure which allows children to sit quietly at the dinner table or to go bed without asking.

Kids fight. That's what they do. Wrestling on the living room floor with a younger brother is a necessary act of socialization This form of play is how they learn boundaries: the limits of their body and the limits of others. Jiu Jitsu gives kids the opportunity to do this in a safe and controlled environment, and to do so with purpose.

We do very specific live training with our youngest age group (4-8 years old) with simple directives. We take the four major positions -- guard, side control, mount, and back -- and focus entirely on control. If you are in a safe spot, keep it. If you are in a bad spot, escape. And then we let them run wild.

I am always blown away by the natural inclination that most kids possess. They know where to go and understand how to get there. With the slightest instruction, these young students actually play Jiu Jitsu. And they can do so with an intensity that most adults cannot, as their young malleable joints and inability to create great force allow for intense training with no adverse health effects. They can truly practice fighting. And then they learn to fight nice.

One of the most profound benefits of Jiu Jitsu is that we are constantly given the opportunity to be in an advantageous position over another and to empathetically practice concern for their well-being. We know what hurts us, so we know what hurts them. We perform joint locks slowly because we've felt the pain when someone does them quickly. We make sure our chokes are on the neck, because we've all felt the discomfort of a white belt squeezing with all their might on our chin.

Jiu Jitsu allows us to daily practice kindness from positions of strength. What a gift for the developing child. Taking care of your partner today means taking care of your fellow employees thirty years from now. They are learning the skills of empathic embrace that come only with the experiences which force empathy. This will translate into better relationships, and therefore a better life, in the future.

When kids learn to fight nice, they get all the physical benefits of fighting without the ramifications. When they learn to exercise concern for others while in positions of dominance, they learn how to lead and love.

The Competence Hierarchy

In Rule #1, we learned about the competence hierarchy: the hundreds of millions of years old system organisms use to organize themselves. To the victor go the spoils, and this has become known as the Matthew Principle:

> "For to every one who has will more be given, and he will have abundance; but from him who has not, even what he has will be taken away."
> - Matthew 25:29, RSV

The organism most suited to excel in its environment, the one at the top of the hierarchy, will receive the best of that environment -- shelter, food, territory, mates. Humans are no different. In each field of human endeavor, the most competent receive the most reward for their efforts.

In Rule 7, Peterson tells of a vision he had:

> "I had a vision, once, of an immense landscape, spread for miles out to the horizon before me. I was high in the air, granted a bird's-eye view. Everywhere I could see great stratified multi-

> storied pyramids of glass, some small, some large, some overlapping, some separate -- all akin to modern skyscrapers; all full of people striving to reach each pyramid's very pinnacle..."

Every one of us exists in such a pyramid. As we ascend the heights of professional success, we get a better office, more money and vacation days. The more competent we become, the more we are given. Competence hierarchies are real. They matter. And without them, humanity crumbles.

Lessons From The Past

> "Human beings are born with different capacities. If they are free, they are not equal. And if they are equal, they are not free."
> - Alexander Solzhenitsyn

Peterson has talked at length about the atrocities of the 20th century that resulted from an abandonment of this universal principle in pursuit of equality of outcome. Using Price's Law and the Pareto Principle, Peterson has continually shown the embodiment of the Matthew Principle. Most book sales go to a handful of authors. Most record sales are by a fraction of artists. Our sun houses most of the mass in the solar system. Once more, consider the board game Monopoly. Everyone starts with an equal amount of resources, but the game always

94

ends with one person having all of them. This happens every time we play. This is the law of distribution and an inherent law of being. Neglecting this truth, chaos ensues.

We have seen the horrors of communism. When we make everyone equal, we must remove their freedom to do so. Rather than pursue equality of outcome, equality of opportunity is the goal. We are all divine. We all deserve an opportunity to manifest our highest potential, and throughout history we have witnessed the suffering which ensues from the negation of this fundamental need.

The competence hierarchy is inescapable. There is a movement these days of participation trophies and safe spaces. We live in a world where college students criticize the ruling class without realizing, as Peterson puts it, that they are "baby ruling class." Rather than complain about the lack of equality in outcomes, we must teach our children to accept the variance of being, carry a worthwhile load, and strive to ascend the hierarchies in which they find themselves in.

Lessons For The Future

"...any hierarchy creates winners and losers... (1) the collective pursuit of any valued goal produces a hierarchy (as some will be better and some worse at that pursuit no matter what it is)

> and (2) it is the pursuit of goals that in large part lends life its sustaining meaning."

Our children exist within competence hierarchies. Those who reach the top of the pyramid have access to more. In Malcolm Gladwell's book *Outliers*, he explains why a staggeringly large portion of NHL players have a birthday in the first quarter of the year. Due to the age cut off for junior leagues, those with birthdays in these months are the oldest within their age group, and in young kids, an age gap of nine months to a year leads to a great disparity in physical development. This advantage leaves these kids more likely to be selected to all-star teams, thus receiving better coaching and more ice time, creating a positive feedback loop in which they progress the fastest, and thus are more likely to continue to make the best teams and have more opportunities. Eventually, more of these young men achieve the highest level of sport (the top of their competence hierarchy) compared to those with fewer advantages.

The same holds true for life. And the same holds true for Jiu Jitsu.

The belt system is a direct representation of the competence hierarchy and with a higher rank comes more opportunity. The senior student leads the line during warm-ups. The senior student has the leadership role to be partnered up with new students and act as assistant coach for the day. They are eligible for advanced classes and thus receive more training. But there is a social aspect that supersedes all of this: being atop the competence hierarchy provides the serotonin boost we all seek.

The Matakas Jiu Jitsu Academy has been open for 7 months at the time of this writing. We have a few junior gray belts. They are at the top of the competence hierarchy among our young students. And everyone knows it. The young students become obsessed with promotions and talk about the junior gray belt constantly. And because we line up rank order to begin and end each class, they are all vying to ascend that line to ultimately be the one that leads the warm-up. They even have little tussles and awkward exchanges as they push and shove to be first.

And all of this is done without any promptings from the instructors on the responsibilities of leadership. I have not consciously articulated to them the value of this position. But they all know it. They all want to be a top their competence hierarchy. And it is this desire that fuels their progress.

In the kids program, you get promoted by doing a few things consistently. Train hard. Take care of your partner. Get good at the techniques. Focus. Be respectful. The students who do this get promoted and ascend the hierarchy. This is perhaps Jiu Jitsu's greatest lesson for these young kids. That if you put in the work toward a worthwhile aim, you are rewarded. They are learning the positive feedback loop of effort and attention. They understand that they exist within a hierarchy and that certain behaviors allow you to ascend that hierarchy. And certain behaviors, hurting others or hurting yourself by not trying, cause you to descend that hierarchy.

Even at four years old, there is a clear distinction between the students who are conscientious and understand these principles and those who do not. They do better on the mat, at home, and in school.

> "In societies that are well-functioning -- not in comparison to a hypothetical utopia, but contrasted with other existing or historical cultures -- competence, not power, is a prime determiner of status."

Jiu Jitsu teaches kids to be competent. The immediate feedback of live training tells them what works and what doesn't. With consistent data, they can make daily improvements. They learn the nature of skill acquisition and the role hierarchies play within a well-structured society. Jiu Jitsu teaches them to fight, and more importantly, to "fight nice." To care for others from positions of power and to remember that their training partner has the same rights, hopes, and feelings that they do.

All of this happens as they finally have an appropriate outlet to use all that potential energy that youth possesses, and to use it in a way that cultivates the development of life skills. The mat provides countless opportunities to learn the value of hard work, to practice concern for the well-being of others, and to realize that competence hierarchies exist, and that they provide benefits proportionate to our ascension.

We are not training children to fight. We are training them to live.

Rule 12
Pet a Cat When You Encounter
One On The Street

In his final rule, Peterson talks in painful depth about the health issues of his daughter, and how his family's misfortunes, like our own, are part of the ineradicable suffering which accompanies Being.

Life is suffering. It was the Buddha's first noble truth. It is demonstrated by the symbolism of Jesus on the cross. To live is to experience pain. Our mission, as Peterson has taught in his lectures, is to accept that pain voluntarily and strive on behalf of the Good, to accept the limitations of being and work for its betterment. And the greater the cross we carry, the more meaning and subsequent resistance to the tragedy of Being we will experience.

We suffer in part because we are limited. But it is this limitation that affords us meaning.

> "Imagine a Being who is omniscient, omnipresent, and omnipotent. What does such a Being lack? The answer? Limitation... it is for this reason, so the story goes, that God created man. No limitation, no story. No story, no Being. That idea has helped me deal with the terrible fragility of Being."

That *story* comes from being vulnerable and risking death -- literally, figuratively, psychologically -- in pursuit of something greater. Consider the archetypal hero story. There is always some great obstacle to be overcome, in which the heroes risk their safety or even existence itself to achieve their holy grail. It is the fragility (limitation) of the hero that makes him or her the hero. Pinocchio risks his life (sort of?) to rescue Geppetto from the belly of the whale. Simba lost his father and had to transition through painful adolescence, struggling upward, to ultimately become capable of defeating Scar. Knights are only knights when dragons present a challenge. Without an obstacle or adversary which forces courage -- risking what you are to become what you could be -- there is no opportunity to be courageous.

In this chapter, Peterson references the evolution of the comic book hero Superman, who was given more and more power overtime by the writers until he became invulnerable. And then the story grew stale as there was no worthwhile struggle in which Superman could engage:

> "A superhero who can do anything turns out to be no hero at all. He's nothing specific, so he's nothing. He has nothing to strive against, so he can't be admirable. Being of any reasonable sort appears to require limitation."

Our limitation is the source of our suffering in this life, but it is also the source of our greatest triumph. It is our weakness that allows us to cultivate true strength.

The Limitation of Adulthood

I am now an adult. I don't know how it happened. Suddenly, I'm 32, a business owner, and all my joints hurt. I've made it! But becoming an adult in this culture comes with certain restrictions.

There are bills to be paid. Keeping a roof over your head, at least a roof of the type we are accustomed to in the western world, costs money. Health insurance. Car insurance. Life insurance. Internet. Cable. 401Ks. Leaky pipes and broken heaters. Taxes. There is much administrative work that comes with aging, along with the decline of bodily functions. There is more to be done but less energy to do it. There are the same sports, but we don't possess the same joints with which to play them.

And when we bear a truly worthwhile cross, like the meaningful relationship with a significant other and having kids, we are suddenly at the mercy of circumstance. To love another more than you love yourself is to be courageous, as we allow our loved one's vulnerability to become our own. To package your well-being with theirs because it's worth it: this is love. And the more meaningful a life you want, the more you leave yourself vulnerable to tragedy and malevolence.

We no longer have rose-tinted glasses. Experience and the news won't let us. In Rule 6, Peterson shares a stat that by June 2016, there had been a mass killing (at least four people shot in single event, not counting the shooter) in the United States on five out of every six days for over three years. This is terrifying, and I am not even a parent. I cannot imagine the anxiety of those with children.

Concern for our loved one's safety is paramount. But that doesn't free us of concern for ourselves. Cancers, heart and metabolic diseases are on the rise. And if we beat those, dementia and Alzheimer's related deteriorations await many of us.

In summary, life is hard. And it may very well get harder. Meaningful engagement protects us from inescapable suffering, as the pursuit of a worthy goal wards off existential and daily concerns. This is the role Jiu Jitsu plays for all of us, acting as a vehicle by which we pursue our highest selves so that we have more to offer those around us. Living according to this meaning will be the focus of our final chapter. But before we close with a dialogue about Jiu Jitsu as a vehicle for personal development, we must first see Jiu Jitsu as a vehicle for play. Because in a life filled with suffering, this is just as important.

Jiu Jitsu As Play

Jiu Jitsu can be the cat on the street, that:

> "Afterward, if she feels like it, she might come visit you, for half a minute. It's a nice break, it's a little extra light, on a good day, and a tiny respite, on a bad day. ...and maybe when you are going for a walk and your head is spinning a cat will show up and if you pay attention to it then you will get a reminder for just about fifteen seconds that the wonder of Being might make up for the ineradicable suffering that accompanies it."

Sometimes we just need a break from our daily experience and the stress of modern life. We need a place to leave our problems at the door, if only for an hour, and be around people who support us as we move and play. Last chapter we discussed the importance of kids doing Jiu Jitsu, for the most basic need of expending energy. Adults share this same requirement. Tension from our stressful lives builds. We need a physical outlet to exhaust that stress before its corrosive effects take hold of our immune system and mental health. We always leave the academy lighter than when we walked in, as the change in our physiology makes the problems of the day seem less daunting.

When such stress builds and I lose my way, I remind myself of the following Zen parable:

A Zen teacher saw five of his students returning from the market, riding their bicycles. When they arrived at the monastery and dismounted their bicycles, the teacher asked the students, "Why are you riding your bicycles?"

The first student said, "It is the bicycle that is carrying the sack of potatoes. I am glad that my back has escaped the pain of bearing the weight." The teacher was glad and said, "You are a smart boy. When you become old, you will be saved of a hunchback, unlike me."

The second student said, "I love to have my eyes over the trees and the sprawling fields as I go riding." The teacher commented, "You have your eyes open and you see the world."

The third student said, "When I ride, I am content to chant affirmations of gratitude." The teacher spoke these words of appreciation, "Your mind will roll with ease like a newly trued wheel."

The fourth student said, "Riding my bicycle I live in perfect harmony of things." The pleased teacher said, "You are actually riding the golden path of non-harming or non-violence."

The fifth student said, "I ride my bicycle to ride my bicycle."

The teacher walked up to him and sat at his feet and said, "I am your student."

The more conscientious we are, the more there is to be learned from this story. It is so easy to become disciplined to the point of losing your humanity. The western mind is always striving toward something, as we emphasize becoming and neglect being. If we spend our whole lives striving for more, we will easily forget the riches we already possess.

Most of my practice has been spent diligently pursuing skill acquisition. Every training session has had a focus. The day was always a success or failure based on my ability to implement a particular technique. So many times, I became manically obsessed with an aspect of Jiu Jitsu and training felt like work. Work I loved, but work. It took me a while to understand the importance of playing Jiu Jitsu. In 5 Rules For White Belts, I discussed that the vocabulary of Jiu Jitsu reveals how it is meant to be performed. We are Jiu Jitsu players, so we should play. It is called "rolling," so we roll like a ball seamlessly through transitions, rather than a bulky cube that topples violently from side to side.

We are meant to play Jiu Jitsu, especially those of us who are not competing. The intense, competition-like training leaves the middle of the bell curve broken and unable to train consistently. Much of the character development that Jiu Jitsu provides can be achieved from training at sub-maximal intensities. And it is at this reduced speed that we are truly able to flow and play, enjoying the roll by rolling ourselves.

Life is hard. Adults have very few outlets in which to play which are conducive to our health. We can play by going to the bar, but then our livers suffer. We can sit idly and watch sports, but our bodies atrophy. These escapes are passive. We are not fully engaged. Jiu Jitsu provides a place to come together to play something that molds our being while freeing us from the pressures of the day.

Peterson encourages the reader to pet a cat when they encounter one on the street. To free you of your troubles, if only for a moment, and to remind you of the joy of Being. This is what Jiu Jitsu can be, if we need it to. Sometimes you are in the spring of your life, all is well, and you have the energy and attention to pursue mastery in this art as you seek to master yourself. But sometimes, the flood comes. You are broken, and the suffering of life seems too much. This is when it's time to play.

Get on the mat, play Jiu Jitsu, and if only for that hour, you can again see the light in the world. We all need to play, no matter our age. Jiu Jitsu gives us that outlet. And sometimes, this is the most valuable aspect of our experience.

Rule 7
Do What Is Meaningful,
Not What Is Expedient

We will address Rule #7 last because I feel it represents the underlying theme of Peterson's *12 Rules* and much of his teachings to date. Do what is meaningful, not what is expedient. Do the things that lead to your betterment and the improvement of the world rather than that which adds to entropy. Aim up instead of down. Make the sacrifices today that will allow you to be better tomorrow. Let go of what you are to become what you could be.

Peterson quotes Wisdom 2:1-11, RSV, which ends:

> "...for what is weak proves itself to be useless."

Peterson has proposed a simple schema through which to interpret experience. We are the exploratory hero acting in a world of order and chaos. We are goal directed creatures, aiming at the desirable future and away from the unbearable present. We see the world subjectively, through the lens of our goal, and thus codify experiences as tools, obstacles, and that which does not matter. While we pursue this goal, we are constantly confronting the varying impulses and drives within our being which vie for the light.

The drives (or sub-personalities) which are not in accordance with our aim weaken our efforts. It is this inherent human weakness which proves itself to be useless. Weakness and expediency often walk hand in hand.

> "Hard choices, easy life. Easy choices, hard life."– Jerzy Gregorek.

Sacrifice And The Delay Of Gratification

A common theme in Peterson's work, certainly in this text, is the idea of sacrifice:

> "People watched the successful succeed and the unsuccessful fail for thousands of years. We thought it over, and drew a conclusion: The successful among us delay gratification. The successful among us bargain with the future."

This, in part, is the source of meaning: engaging in practices that align with our aim and bring us closer to its actualization. We all come to Jiu Jitsu for different reasons. But we all come for the same reason: To improve, to use this art as a tool for personal development and grow in the ways we most need. This requires sacrifice.

In pursuing what we wish to become, we must let go of all that does not serve this aim. I recently had two students tell me that after a lifetime of smoking they were finally quitting. They both began Jiu Jitsu within the last month and now saw a direct reflection between their habits off the mat and their experiences on the mat. The pleasure of smoking was no longer worth the exhaustion of training. They were now willing to sacrifice that habit, to let that piece of them die off, so that they may become something greater.

Jiu Jitsu forces us, out of love for the art, to do what is optimal for ourselves. We can no longer eat junk food or stay up late. An early Friday night means good Saturday morning training. Jiu Jitsu becomes the meaningful which takes the place of the expedient. Netflix loses its appeal. So does the bar. We start to see these things for what they are, distractions packaged in the guise of easy choices which lead to a less meaningful life.

The more love we develop for the art, the more love we show ourselves. Because to embody the Jiu Jitsu lifestyle, to make the sacrifices that allow us to develop within the art, we must let go of many of the prescriptions of western society.

We are made free of our weakness by binding ourselves to something worthwhile.

For many, Jiu Jitsu is our first experience delaying gratification in adult life. We work our jobs and pay our bills, just trying to make it day by day. Our stressful lives need decompression, a release we often find in tasty foods or on big screens. But the more time we spend on the mat, struggling toward a worthy ideal, the less need we have for such things. They no longer satisfy us because we are living a more meaningful life. We begin by sacrificing these pleasures for our practice of the art. It's only later that we come to see these pleasures for what they are: a sacrifice of our ideal self.

Every action moves us closer or further from who we want to become. Peterson has talked about Jung's idea that the Self, you in your totality across time, beckons you forth through meaning. That meaning is how you orient yourself in life. And the more meaningful something is, the more you are willing to trade for its fulfillment. Jiu Jitsu gives us a reason to let go of expediency in exchange for something worthwhile. It gives us the tools to strive and grow beyond ourselves, toward whatever highest self awaits. It is something different for all of us. But it is the same for each of us.

It is the vehicle by which we become more. And we become more so we have more to give.

Embody the Archetype

Peterson references the bible repeatedly in *12 Rules*. And for good reason. The world is a forum for action as well as a place of things. Science tells you what is but cannot tell you how to act from objective facts. This is where religion and mythology come in. They inform us how to act in the world. They are the blueprint to navigate reality and structure your existence in a way which is good for you, those around you, and your world. When describing Christ, he says:

> "That is the archetypal story of the man who gives his all for the sake of the better -- who offers up his life for the advancement of Being -- who allows God's will to become manifest within the confines of a single, mortal life."

Who gives his all for the sake of the better, and who strives to become more so that he can serve others. We are each connected. And when we improve our lives through Jiu Jitsu, we improve the lives of everyone around us. A dad has a productive outlet for the stress at work and can now be more present with his kids at home. A mom loses weight through training and feels the physical confidence that she lost since her youth. The young boy or girl who learns that with great power comes great responsibility and chooses to stand up to bullies rather than be one. Each takes something different away from Jiu Jitsu. And the lives of all with whom they interact are improved as a result.

Every hero story follows the same path. The hero leaves the regular world to confront a great challenge. He or she is then transformed into something greater because of their struggle. They return home with more to offer their community.

This is what each of us does with our time in Jiu Jitsu. By pursuing what has meaning, we daily strive toward personal development, and the depth of our journey is matched by the positive influence we have on those around us. In the last chapter we discussed the idea of the competence hierarchy, quoting Peterson:

> "I had a vision, once, of an immense landscape, spread for miles out to the horizon before me. I was high in the air, granted a bird's-eye view. Everywhere I could see great stratified multi-storied pyramids of glass, some small, some large, some overlapping, some separate -- all akin to modern skyscrapers; all full of people striving to reach each pyramid's very pinnacle..."

We each strive to the top of our respective pyramids. When we reach the top, we win the game. But there is another game, a meta-game, a more real game, which exists beyond the confines of our personal pursuits. The passage continues:

> "But there was something above that pinnacle, a domain outside each pyramid, in which all were nested. That was the privileged position of the eye that could or perhaps chose to soar freely above the fray; that chose not to dominate any specific group or cause but instead to somehow simultaneously transcend all."

This is the viewpoint of the humanist, the servant who strives on behalf of humanity for the betterment of Being. This is what it means to use Jiu Jitsu as a vehicle for personal development. Mastery of the art is one pyramid. And it is one worth striving to ascend. But this is nested within something far greater, the advancement of your individual experience to heighten your quality of life and the lives of those around you. To mistake mastery of Jiu Jitsu as the end is to miss the mark. We too often identify with the vehicle and forget it is a vessel by which we move down the road of life toward the destination of our highest selves.

Who we become matters far more than any guard pass. But we use the guard passes, and the discipline, effort, and attention they require, to get there.

There is nothing more meaningful than human relationships. Two summers ago, I went on a solo road trip to many of the national parks. I had to get away and reassess the purpose of my life. While away, I realized that though nature was beautiful, solitude in the mountains did not provide the same meaning as human interaction. We are here for each other. And the worth of our actions is proportionate to the betterment of Being they bring forth.

Referencing the followers of Christ, Peterson says:

> "This imitation was the sacred duty of the believer not to adhere (or merely to mouth) a set of statements about abstract belief but instead to actually manifest the spirit of the Savior in the particular, specific conditions of his or her life - - to realize or incarnate the archetype..."

I have studied personal development since college. I have done so with as much sincerity and attention as I can muster. I have found no better example of how to live than the ideal set by Christ. This remains true independent of the historical truth of the doctrine, whether he is a story, a man, or God.

But I could never clearly codify what it meant to live by this example; I knew it but could not articulate it. Aldous Huxley described this perennial philosophy through the vocabulary of the Sermon on the Mount, stating that we are to become loving, pure in heart and poor in spirit.

This was closer to the approximation of my aim, but it wasn't enough. Then Peterson published a video for Easter of 2018, *The Death and Resurrection of Christ: A Commentary in Five Parts*, in which he describes the axioms of embodying this archetype. The first five read:

> 1) To decide that and enact the proposition that Being is Good, despite its tragedy and malevolence.
>
> 2) To work, in consequence, for the continual and eternal improvement of that Being, and to know that as Love.
>
> 3) To do such work in Truth.

4) To let everything inadequate burn off in that pursuit, and to welcome its replacement by what is better.

5) To know that as the sacred Imitation of Christ.

The world redeemer myth has never been so clearly articulated. Seen through a pragmatic and humanist lens, outside of theology, I believe these precepts describe our optimal mode of being, as living according to its dictates fosters proper action and imbues our lives with meaning.

I can't help but notice how similar this axiomatic system is to the nature of Jiu Jitsu.

We accept the difficulty of the task. We suffer willingly toward our own development. We fall in love with the pursuit of constant improvement. Jiu Jitsu strips us bare and reveals us to ourselves. We cannot hide. We are naked. With this conscious understanding of what we are, we let die off whatever doesn't serve us. We strive to become more. And in our growth, we become better for those around us. We now have more to give, and we give it with love.

Jiu Jitsu has been compared to a religion. Sometimes to a cult. And we "followers" certainly become evangelical in our practice. For good reason. We have found a discipline that gives our life meaning. We want to share it with others. But even if our loved ones never

116

step foot inside the academy, we still share the gentle art with them. By allowing the art to mold us, we become the conduit through which Jiu Jitsu improves the lives of those who have never stepped foot on the mat.

Meaning

We saved this rule for last because I believe it to be the underlying theme of all of Peterson's work. The course of my life has been changed by his teachings. For nearly two years, every car ride, meal, and idle time has been spent listening to his lectures. They are gold. They are a culmination of the best wisdom of the humanities taught through a psychological lens with a pragmatic application. His dictum "Clean your Room" has become part of the lexicon of this generation. The role of the individual is to start with themselves. Improve the things you can improve. Strive for the Good. Become more. And with your newfound strength and ability, contribute to the world in a positive way.

I have been practicing Jiu Jitsu for a decade. I have only begun to explore the significance of this discipline. I hope to someday be capable of describing this significance with words deserving of the art. Jiu Jitsu is a gift. The more sincerely we seek to understand and master the art, our lives grow in proportion. It is a vehicle through which we mold ourselves. An environment which sheds our weakness and forces our adaptation into resilient, hardworking, and attentive students. Jiu Jitsu makes us better. And it makes us kinder. When we learn we are not made of glass, we no longer feel the need to prove it to the world. We are free of ourselves by strengthening ourselves.

By becoming more, we have more to offer the world. Peterson's teachings aid in this process. He, too, is a gift to humanity. And I can't help but read his words and see the direct correlation to Jiu Jitsu. All his axioms on how to live apply directly to the practice of the gentle art. Together, they are part of a much larger curriculum.

In his biblical series, he references Christ's injunction from the Sermon on the Mount that the "meek shall inherit the earth." He explains that the original meaning of the word "meek" translates to those who can wield a sword but keep it sheathed. This is Jiu Jitsu. We develop a great capacity for violence and the moral education to abstain from using our abilities. We develop a strength that allows us to be gentle. And in our gentleness, we express true strength.

We are all part of something bigger than ourselves. It is a lot easier to make things worse than to make them better. To improve yourself and your world takes time. It is a ceaseless struggle to overcome our natural weakness and strive for that heavenly city on the hill. None of us has scratched the surface of what we could be. And there is no way to tell the effect that we can have on the world, if we struggle toward a worthy ideal for a lifetime, working for the betterment of Being.

Jiu Jitsu is the tool by which we mold ourselves. It frees us from expediency and gives us greater meaning. Jiu Jitsu gives us the opportunity to become what we might be, training our soul as we embody the spirit of the archetype.

Jiu Jitsu is the vehicle. The pyramid of competence which we all seek to ascend. But there exists a far deeper, richer mode of being, above and beyond this discipline. It is this discipline, however, that reveals it.

Made in the USA
Las Vegas, NV
10 December 2020